# HEAL SISTER HEAL

## A Sister's Guide to Wholeness

*By*
ADAWNA BELL, LMFT

HEAL SISTER HEAL

*A Sister's Guide to Wholeness*

Copyright © 2024 by Adawna Bell.

ISBN: 979-8-9894463-4-6

All rights reserved. No part of this book may be reproduced or transmitted in any form or by any means without written permission from the author.

Build A Brother Publishing.

# DEDICATION

This book is dedicated to the ladies of Heal Sister Heal. The way you embraced the idea of our Heal Sister Heal group was unimaginable. The laughter we have shared over the years plus your love and encouragement means the world to me. I hope this book continues to help us all on our healing journey.

*Adawna*

# CONTENTS

| | |
|---|---:|
| INTRODUCTION | 1 |
| CHAPTER 1: Uplift Your Sister | 5 |
| CHAPTER 2: Take That S Off Your Chest | 13 |
| CHAPTER 3: You're More Than Enough | 21 |
| CHAPTER 4: It's OK to Rest | 29 |
| CHAPTER 5: God Hears You | 35 |
| CHAPTER 6: Doubt Your Doubts and Let Go of Your Shoulds | 43 |
| CHAPTER 7: Go After Your Dreams | 53 |
| CHAPTER 8: Healed And Healing | 63 |
| EXERCISES | 71 |
| ABOUT THE AUTHOR | 97 |

# INTRODUCTION

Welcome, dear reader, to "Heal Sister Heal," a sanctuary in words, designed to guide you through the personal landscapes of healing and self-discovery. This book is a lovingly crafted collection of self-help exercises, insights, and reflections intended to support you as you navigate the complexities of your unique healing journey. Whether you are mending from past pain, seeking to grow beyond current challenges, or simply aiming to enhance your overall well-being, this book is your companion.

In the following pages, you will encounter a variety of exercises aimed at fostering emotional, physical, and spiritual growth. These exercises are not just activities but invitations—to dig deeper, reach higher, and stretch further into the essence of who you are. Each one is crafted with the intent to help you embrace the new and let go of the old, supporting you in shedding those layers that no longer serve you.

Why "Heal Sister Heal"? Because healing is not merely about moving past your pain; it's about stepping into your power. It is about transforming your trials into triumphs, your wounds into wisdom. This book embraces the idea that every woman is her own best healer, that within you lies the capacity to mend what is

## INTRODUCTION

broken, to right what is wronged, and to rise above what has tried to defeat you.

Healing is a marathon, not a sprint. It is a series of small steps that lead to grand transformations. It requires patience, persistence, and most importantly, compassion for oneself. Each chapter of this book is designed to encourage these virtues and to remind you that while the journey is yours alone, you do not walk it without support.

From learning to say "no" to embracing physical activity, from practicing mindfulness to engaging in creative expression, the exercises provided here are meant to be practical, manageable, and adaptable. They will challenge you to confront uncomfortable truths, to dismantle unhelpful patterns, and to build healthier habits. The journey of healing is personal and profound, and this book aims to honor that sacred endeavor.

As you turn these pages, remember that each word was chosen with a heartfelt desire to see you grow and thrive. The world needs your healed self, your whole self, your unabashedly vibrant self. So, dear sister, as you embark on this journey of healing, do so with the knowledge that you are capable, you are deserving, and you are not alone.

Heal, sister, heal. Not just because you need it, but because the world benefits immeasurably from your light. When Genevieve first approached me to co-found this movement with her, we had no clue that this journey would lead us here. Let this book be your guide, your reminder, and your encouragement. Here's to healing, to growing, and to becoming the very best version of yourself. Welcome to your healing journey. Let it be profound, let it be joyful, let it be thoroughly transformative. Let's begin.

"You may not always have a comfortable life and you will not always be able to solve all of the world's problems at once but don't ever underestimate the importance you can have because history has shown us that courage can be contagious and hope can take on a life of its own."

— MICHELLE OBAMA

## CHAPTER 1

# Uplift Your Sister

Do you realize how magical we are as black women? Historically we have always been magical. We can nurture our children, love our husbands, go to school, work, start a business, and uplift other women. We can say something to a woman that makes her feel amazing about herself. However, we can also say something to another woman that makes her feel like she is the worst person in the world. Which one are you? Are you the woman who compliments another woman, even a total stranger? You know what I'm speaking about. "You're working those heels girl!" "I see you polka dots!" "You better wear that purple girl! You never know how those words can impact another woman. Especially one that may be having a bad day. It doesn't matter if the woman is a teenage girl, a woman in her 30's, 50's or 90's! Your words of encouragement may be the best words she hears that day. On the other hand, you can use your words to cause harm. "Oh, she thinks she's cute"! "You think you're all that." The truth is, she doesn't think she's all that, YOU DO. Something about her confidence bothers you. That woman who stirs up your insecurity does not realize she's doing that. She's just living her life. Just like positive words can give her life, negative words can be what breaks her down. What is it about her that is triggering the mean girl inside of you? Whatever it is, that is not her problem. It's yours and yours alone. It is also your responsibility to work on your healing.

Once you're comfortable, then use it on other women. Imagine a world where every woman realizes her true potential and harnesses her unique magic for good. As black women, our journey has not been easy, but it has been filled with resilience, strength, and unparalleled grace. Our history is replete with stories of struggle, but also of triumph. From overcoming the chains of slavery to breaking barriers in various fields, our ancestors have laid a strong foundation for us to build upon. The magic of black women is not just in our ability to overcome adversity but also in our innate ability to inspire and empower others. When we uplift one another, we create a ripple effect of positivity and strength that can transform communities. Our words have power, and when used positively, they can help heal wounds, build confidence, and inspire dreams.

It's essential to remember that our magic isn't just about what we say, but also about what we do. Our actions, big or small, can have a significant impact. Whether it's mentoring a young girl, supporting a local black-owned business, standing up against injustice, or simply being a source of comfort and support to a friend in need, every action contributes to the collective strength and magic of our community. Moreover, embracing our individuality is a crucial part of unlocking our magic. As black women, we are not a monolith; we come in all shapes, sizes, colors, and from various backgrounds. Our diversity is our strength, and when we embrace and celebrate our differences, we set a powerful example for the world. It's about owning our stories, our struggles, and our triumphs, and using them to empower ourselves and others. We also need to recognize the importance of self-care in nurturing our magic. As caretakers, professionals, and community leaders, we often put others before ourselves. However, it's vital to remember that we cannot pour from an empty cup. Taking care of our physical, mental, and emotional well-being is not selfish; it's necessary. When we are at our best, we are more capable of being a positive force in the lives of others.

In the face of adversity, our magic becomes even more crucial. In times of social and political turmoil, when our rights and dignity are under attack, our collective magic can be a powerful tool for change. By standing together, supporting one another, and using our voices and talents, we can fight for justice and equality. Our magic lies in our resilience, our ability to hope, and our unyielding spirit. Finally, it's important to pass on our magic to the next generation. Our daughters, nieces, and young girls in our community look up to us. They learn from our actions, our words, and our attitudes. By setting a positive example, we can instill in them the values of kindness, empathy, confidence, and resilience. We can teach them to love themselves, to embrace their unique magic, and to use it to make the world a better place. The magic of black women is a potent force that can transform lives and communities. It's about using our words and actions to uplift others, embracing our diversity, taking care of ourselves, standing up against injustice, and inspiring the next generation. Let's continue to harness our magic, not just for ourselves, but for the betterment of our world.

Remember, when one of us shines, we all shine brighter together. Once you're healed and healing, you unlock your magic. We don't know what another woman is going through. Why not use your magic to uplift the next woman? It won't take away from your magic, it will only add to it. Teach your daughters how to use their magic positively. If no one ever taught you how to use your magic, try it on yourself first. Once you're comfortable, then use it on other women. The world does a really good job of causing black women pain, we don't have to do it to each other. When we uplift another woman, we are also uplifting ourselves. Let's empower each other by cultivating confidence. I was at an event a few months ago with some beauty queens and I made the mistake of saying I am not a queen. All of those wonderful women said immediately, "Yes You Are!" That's empowering. We uplift each other by encouraging and validating each other. We empower by making room for mistakes and for making room for learning. We uplift by teaching younger women and hopefully, they won't make the same mistakes. They will see other women as their contemporaries and not their adversaries.

Here are some helpful tips for you, inspired by this chapter:

1. **Practice Positive Affirmations**: Start your day with positive affirmations. This can boost your self-esteem and set a positive tone for your day. For example, affirm your strength, beauty, and intelligence. This practice reinforces a positive self-image and can also encourage you to spread positivity to others.
2. **Empower Through Compliments**: Make a conscious effort to compliment other women. Whether it's a colleague, a friend, or a stranger, a genuine compliment can have a lasting impact on someone's day and self-esteem.
3. **Develop Self-awareness**: Reflect on your words and actions and how they affect others. If you find yourself feeling envious or negative towards another woman, take a moment to understand why and work towards turning those feelings into something constructive.
4. **Embrace and Celebrate Diversity**: Recognize and celebrate the differences among women in your community. Organize or participate in events that highlight and embrace diverse cultures, backgrounds, and experiences.
5. **Mentorship and Support**: If possible, become a mentor to younger or less experienced women. Sharing your knowledge and experience can be incredibly empowering for both you and the mentee.
6. **Promote Self-care**: Prioritize your well-being. Remember, taking care of yourself enables you to take care of

others more effectively. This includes physical health, mental health, and emotional well-being.
7. **Educate and Learn**: Continuously educate yourself on issues affecting women, especially those from different backgrounds than your own. This broadens your understanding and equips you to be a more effective ally and supporter.
8. **Support Women-led Initiatives**: Whether it's a local business, a community project, or an online platform, supporting women-led initiatives helps strengthen the collective power and influence of women.
9. **Encourage Open Dialogue**: Foster environments where women feel safe to share their experiences and challenges. This can be in the workplace, social circles, or family settings.
10. **Advocate for Equality**: Stand up against injustice and inequality in your community. Use your voice and platform, no matter how big or small, to advocate for the rights and equal treatment of women.
11. **Pass on Your Knowledge**: Share your experiences, lessons, and insights with the younger generation. This can be through informal conversations, writing, or participating in community programs.

By integrating these tips into daily life, women can actively contribute to a more supportive, empowering, and inclusive community.

"I can be changed by what happens to me, but I refuse to be reduced by it."

— MAYA ANGELOU

## CHAPTER 2
# Take That S Off Your Chest

In the late 80's, Karyn White had a song called "Superwoman". There were so many women who resonated with that song. We are trying to be everything to everyone. Our family, friends, employers, THE WORLD. So many people that we don't take care of ourselves. The "superwoman" title is supposed to be a compliment, but it's an anchor that can and has held many women down. It's time for us to take the S off, and replace it with vulnerability, self-care, boundaries, authenticity, and strong support networks. Black women have been adorned with an invisible "S" on their chests. The "S" symbolizes strength, resilience, and an unwavering ability to endure. While trying to be strong we forget that we can also be vulnerable. I know, I know so many black women hate that word. Why? What is so wrong with being vulnerable? For many women, they were never allowed to be vulnerable. Let's change that. Being vulnerable is not being weak, it's being real. Allowing yourself and the women in your lives to be vulnerable offers a safe space that we don't always have. Allowing vulnerability is just the start. Alongside embracing our true selves, it's crucial to prioritize self-care. The concept of self-care has often been misunderstood or dismissed as mere indulgence, but it's far more than that. It's about giving ourselves the necessary time and space to recharge, reflect, and rejuvenate. This can mean different things for different people: for some, it's a quiet evening with a book; for others, it's an afternoon at the spa or a vigorous workout. The key is to listen to what your body and mind need, recognizing that this is not selfishness, but essential maintenance for our well-being.

Setting boundaries is another critical aspect of shedding the "Superwoman" cape. Boundaries allow us to define where our limits lie, what we are comfortable with, and how we wish to be treated by others. They are the foundation of mutual respect in any relationship, whether personal or professional. Yet, for many Black women, setting boundaries can feel like an uphill battle, given societal expectations to always accommodate and care for others. It's time to challenge these norms and assert our right to personal space, time, and respect. Authenticity is our next piece of armor. Living authentically means being true to ourselves, our values, and our beliefs, even when they go against the grain. It's about owning our stories, our successes, and our struggles, without fear of judgment. This authenticity can be liberating, but it also requires courage, especially in environments that may not always celebrate our unique identities. Yet, the freedom that comes from living authentically is unmatched, offering a profound sense of peace and fulfillment. The importance of a strong support network cannot be overstated. This network includes friends, family, mentors, and peers who understand, uplift, and empower us. A strong support system provides not just emotional comfort, but also practical advice, solidarity, and sometimes a much-needed reality check. In the journey toward self-empowerment, these relationships are invaluable, offering a mirror to our own strength and resilience.

However, as we embrace vulnerability, self-care, boundaries, authenticity, and strong support networks, it's crucial to recognize the societal barriers that may impede this journey. Systemic racism, sexism, and economic disparities disproportionately affect Black women, complicating the path to self-realization and empowerment. Acknowledging these challenges is not an act of concession but a call to action. It highlights the need for systemic change, both within and beyond our communities. Advocating for this change requires collective effort. It involves challenging stereotypes, dismantling structural barriers, and creating inclusive spaces where Black women can thrive. It's about amplifying our voices, sharing our stories, and advocating for policies that address the unique challenges we face. This advocacy is not just for ourselves but for future generations of Black women who deserve a world that recognizes and celebrates their full humanity.

While the "Superwoman" syndrome has been a source of pride, it's time to redefine what strength looks like for Black women. It's about embracing our vulnerability, prioritizing our well-being, setting healthy boundaries, living authentically, and building strong support networks. Self-care is very important. I am not talking about the big things like vacations, spa days, etc. I am also talking about the small things like naps, reading a book, going to the beach, getting a coffee or a milkshake, the gym, and even going to the grocery store alone, All of this is self-care. You deserve to do something for yourself without being made to feel guilty by anyone, including yourself. Taking care of or nurturing yourself is loving yourself. It's not selfish, it's necessary. Taking the S off of your chest is a form of self-care. These steps are not signs of weakness but of profound strength and self-awareness. As we navigate this journey, let's remember to extend grace to ourselves and others. The path to empowerment is not linear; it's filled with ups and downs. But with each step, we're not just shedding the weight of unrealistic expectations; we're also paving the way for a more inclusive, empathetic, and equitable future.

I tell women all the time that "no is a complete sentence". Being able to say no and establishing boundaries is another way of taking the S off. If you tell someone 'no' a few things will happen.

1. They will get angry, but get over it.
2. They will find someone else to do it.
3. They will do it themself.

Either way, once you say no, it is no longer on you to figure out. Always stand on your boundaries and don't allow anyone to ignore them. Be your authentic self. That is the gift you give to the world. It is time for women, especially black women to embrace their multifaceted identity. This includes joys, complexities, and passions. We should never allow society to take away who we are to make them comfortable, because, in the end, we pay. Let's take off the "S" and embrace our multifaceted identities, knowing that our strength lies not in being superwomen, but in being unapologetically ourselves. In doing so, we not only liberate ourselves but also inspire those around us to do the same. The legacy of Black women is one of resilience, creativity, and profound strength. Let's honor that legacy by redefining what it means to be strong, on our own terms.

Here are some helpful tips for you, inspired by the themes discussed in this chapter:

1. **Embrace Vulnerability**: See vulnerability as a strength, not a weakness. Allow yourself to be open about your feelings, fears, and dreams. This can lead to deeper connections with others and a greater sense of self-awareness.

2. **Prioritize Self-Care**: Make self-care a non-negotiable part of your daily routine. Whether it's exercise, meditation, hobbies, or simply quiet time, find what rejuvenates you and make time for it. Remember, self-care is essential, not selfish.

3. **Set Healthy Boundaries**: Learn to say no and set clear boundaries to protect your time, energy, and emotional

well-being. It's crucial for maintaining healthy relationships and a balanced life.

4. **Live Authentically**: Be true to yourself in all aspects of life. Celebrate your unique identity, and don't be afraid to stand out. Authenticity attracts genuine connections and opportunities.

5. **Build a Support Network**: Cultivate a strong network of friends, family, and mentors who uplift and support you. Surround yourself with people who encourage your growth and remind you of your worth.

6. **Recognize and Challenge Systemic Barriers**: Educate yourself on the systemic challenges that impact women, especially Black women, and engage in activism to challenge these issues. Support policies and initiatives that promote equity and justice.

7. **Advocate for Change**: Use your voice and platform to advocate for changes that benefit women in your community and beyond. Whether it's through social media, community organizing, or personal conversations, your advocacy can make a difference.

8. **Practice Self-Compassion**: Be kind to yourself, especially during difficult times. Recognize that it's okay to have off days and that perfection is an unrealistic standard.

9. **Seek Professional Help When Needed**: Don't hesitate to seek support from a therapist or counselor when

dealing with emotional or mental health challenges. Professional help can provide valuable tools and perspectives.

10. **Invest in Continuous Learning**: Always be open to learning—about yourself, others, and the world. Education is a powerful tool for personal growth and empowerment.

11. **Celebrate Your Achievements**: Take time to acknowledge and celebrate your achievements, no matter how small. Recognizing your progress can boost your confidence and motivation.

12. **Engage in Community Service**: Find ways to give back to your community. Helping others can provide a sense of purpose and connect you with like-minded individuals.

By incorporating these tips into your life, you can navigate the complexities of modern womanhood with grace, resilience, and empowerment. Remember, your journey is unique, and embracing your individual path is key to unlocking your full potential.

"Caring for myself is not self-indulgence, it is self-preservation, and that is an act of political warfare."

— AUDRE LORDE

## CHAPTER 3
# You're More Than Enough

My dear sisters. I know the world will tell us that everything we are is not "good enough". Our hair, our bodies, The way we walk, talk, dress, our skin complexion, and even the way we love ourselves and others. If that were true, why are so many other women trying to emulate us? We are brilliant, passionate, nurturing, loving, and quite frankly a force of nature. Who else can make something out of nothing and turn it into everything and more? Forget the stereotypes and standards that don't capture who you are. Don't allow yourself to be defined by others' expectations and standards for you. Standards they don't inspire to. I am not saying standards and expectations aren't important, because they are. However, only your standards and expectations for your life are what matters and no one else's. Your dreams and aspirations are what matters. Your voice is powerful, and your presence shifts rooms.

The question that I ask is why do others go out of their way to make us feel that all we are equal to nothing at all? My guess is due to jealousy, insecurity, fear, and ignorance. Notice I said others. Because men can make us feel terrible about ourselves every bit as much as a woman can. Instead of trying to understand why other people attempt to make you feel bad about yourself, embrace who you are, your identity, fierceness, and your limitless potential. Celebrate yourself and all of your accomplishments. Celebrate your failures too. How else will you learn if you don't fail sometimes?

In other words sis,

YOU ARE MORE THAN ENOUGH!

This statement isn't just a mantra; it's a profound truth that we must internalize and live by. The journey to self-acceptance and empowerment is not an easy one, especially in a world that often seeks to diminish our light. But remember, it's our inner strength, our culture, and our unwavering spirit that have carried us through the toughest of times. It's this very resilience that makes us extraordinary.

Let's talk about the beauty of our uniqueness. Our hair, a crown of diverse textures, defies gravity and society's narrow beauty standards. Our skin, in every shade of melanin, glows with the richness of history, resilience, and beauty that no cosmetic can replicate. Our bodies, diverse and strong, carry us through life's challenges with grace. And our love, deep and unyielding, has the power to heal wounds and bridge divides. Embrace these attributes, for they are your superpowers. Moreover, our contributions to culture, innovation, and society are immeasurable. From the arts to sciences, politics to business, black women have been trailblazers, setting standards of excellence while breaking down barriers. Our creativity and intelligence have sparked movements, built empires, and changed the course of history. Yet, our achievements often go unrecognized, our stories untold. It's time to reclaim our narrative and celebrate our contributions, both big and small.

In facing the world's attempts to make us feel less than, it's vital to cultivate a community of support. Surround yourself with individuals who uplift you, who see your value, and encourage your growth. There is power in unity, in shared experiences, and in collective healing. Together, we can create spaces of empowerment, understanding, and love that counteract the negativity we often face. It's a radical act of self-love that allows us to replenish our energy, nurture our well-being, and maintain our inner peace. Whether it's through meditation, exercise, pursuing hobbies, or simply saying no to overcommitment, prioritize your well-being. Remember, you cannot pour from an empty cup. Taking care of yourself enables you to continue being the force of nature that you are.

Additionally, use your voice and platform, no matter how big or small, to advocate for change. Speak out against injustice, challenge stereotypes, and support causes that uplift black women. Your voice can inspire change, support others in their journey, and contribute to a more equitable and just world.

Embracing your identity also means celebrating your culture and heritage. Dive deep into the history of black women, understand the legacies of those who came before us, and carry forward their spirit of resilience and empowerment. Our history is a tapestry of strength, creativity, and triumph in the face of adversity. Let it remind you of your inherent greatness.

Moreover, do not shy away from failure. Embrace it as a valuable teacher. Each setback is a step forward, a lesson learned that brings you closer to your goals. It's through challenges that we grow stronger, more resilient, and more determined. Celebrate your failures as much as your successes, for they are all part of your journey. Remember to dream big. Your aspirations and goals are valid. Pursue them with passion and determination, knowing that you have within you the power to achieve anything you set your mind to. Break the mold, set new standards, and be the architect of your future.

My dear sisters, know that you are more than enough. You are a testament to the strength, beauty, and brilliance of black womanhood. Let no one dim your light. Embrace your uniqueness, celebrate your achievements, uplift those around you, and continue to break barriers. Your presence is a gift to the world, and your potential is limitless. Stand tall, walk with confidence, and wear your crown with pride. The world needs what you have to offer, so shine brightly, for you are truly a force of nature.

Here are some helpful tips for you, inspired by the empowering themes in this chapter:

1. **Embrace Your Uniqueness**: Celebrate the qualities that make you unique. Whether it's your hair texture, skin color, or personal style, each aspect of your identity is something to take pride in.
2. **Cultivate a Supportive Community**: Surround yourself with people who uplift and support you. A strong support network can provide encouragement, advice, and comfort through life's ups and downs.
3. **Prioritize Self-Care**: Make self-care a non-negotiable part of your routine. Whether it's taking time for activities you love, practicing mindfulness, or ensuring you get enough rest, caring for yourself is crucial.
4. **Use Your Voice for Advocacy**: Speak out against injustices and champion causes that matter to you. Your voice is powerful—use it to effect change and uplift others.
5. **Celebrate Your Achievements and Failures**: Recognize and celebrate your successes, but also embrace your failures as opportunities for growth. Each experience is a stepping stone on your path.
6. **Invest in Your Growth**: Never stop learning and growing. Whether through formal education, personal

reading, or new experiences, continuous learning enriches your life and expands your horizons.
7. **Practice Resilience**: Life will have its challenges, but your response to these obstacles defines your journey. Cultivate resilience by facing difficulties with courage and determination.
8. **Cultivate Financial Independence**: Educate yourself about personal finance and strive for financial independence. Financial empowerment is a key aspect of personal freedom and security.
9. **Seek Out Mentors**: Look for mentors who inspire you and can offer guidance based on their own experiences. A mentor can provide valuable insights, advice, and encouragement.
10. **Care for Your Mental Health**: Pay attention to your mental health. Don't hesitate to seek professional help when needed, and practice strategies that contribute to your mental well-being.
11. **Foster Authentic Connections**: Build genuine relationships based on trust, respect, and mutual support. Authentic connections can provide a sense of belonging and community.
12. **Embrace Leadership Opportunities**: Take on leadership roles when possible. Leading can help you develop new skills, build confidence, and make a positive impact on others.

13. **Celebrate Your Culture and Heritage**: Take pride in your cultural heritage. Understanding and celebrating your roots can provide a strong sense of identity and belonging.
14. **Live Authentically**: Stay true to yourself in all aspects of life. Living authentically brings peace and fulfillment and allows you to live in alignment with your values and beliefs.
15. **Dream Big and Take Action**: Allow yourself to dream big and pursue your aspirations with passion. Set goals and take actionable steps toward achieving them. Remember, your potential is limitless.

These tips are designed to inspire and guide women toward a life of empowerment, resilience, and fulfillment. Remember, the journey is as unique as you are, and embracing your individual path with courage and confidence is the key to unlocking your full potential.

"We realize the importance of our voices only when we are silenced."

— MALALA YOUSAFZAI

## CHAPTER 4
# It's OK to Rest

Let's face it, adulting is not what we thought it would be. I don't know about you but I thought it would be much more fun. When you add on being a wife, mother, daughter, sister, friend, employee, employer, and a decent human being we should all be exhausted. The problem is that we as women do so much for everyone else that we forget to rest. Not just physically but also emotionally. Now some of you might say, I sleep 8 hours a day and can take a nap at the drop of a hat. That's great and quite honestly, I am envious. I am not talking about sleeping, I am talking about resting. There is a difference in the two. Have you ever slept all night and woke up tired? That usually means you didn't rest. Resting means not doing what you have to do all the time. I get it's hard to rest especially if you're a mom to little ones. Here is the trick if you have kids, when they rest you rest. I can hear some women saying, "But that's when I get things done". Those things will still be there if you take some time for yourself. Rest can take many forms. It can be a soak in the tub, reading a book, sitting and doing absolutely nothing, going to bed at a more reasonable time, it can also be going to the beach if you live near one. It's time to normalize resting without guilt. It's part of self-care. We carry many titles, but the most important one is the title "Me". That means this, "if I don't take care of me, who will take care of them? No one will take care of your family (spouse, kids, parents, extended family) the way you do if something happens to you. With that in mind, you must rest. For those of you with daughters, do you want them to emulate you running themselves into the ground or taking a break and resting when needed? Somehow along the way, society tries to make a woman feel guilty for resting. We are not the energizer bunny that just keeps going and going. When you catch a cold, do you take meds and keep going or do you take meds and rest? Most women take meds and keep going. The cold doesn't get better when we keep going. It only gets better when we stop to rest. Our bodies know when we need to rest, we just have to listen. Not just when we're ill but anytime our mind or body says to rest.

The critical lesson here is learning to listen to ourselves—to really tune in to what our bodies and minds are telling us. Too often, we ignore these signals, pushing through fatigue, stress, and even physical discomfort because we feel there's too much to do and too many people relying on us. But this approach isn't sustainable and can lead to burnout, a state of emotional, physical, and mental exhaustion caused by excessive and prolonged stress.

It's time we start treating rest as essential, not optional. Rest isn't just a luxury; it's a fundamental part of maintaining our health and well-being. Here are some strategies to help integrate meaningful rest into our hectic lives:

1. **Establish Boundaries**: One of the most effective ways to ensure you get the rest you need is to set clear boundaries. This might mean saying no to additional responsibilities, delegating tasks at home or work, or simply informing your family of your need for uninterrupted downtime. Boundaries help manage others' expectations and allow you to carve out necessary personal space.
2. **Create a Restful Environment**: Make your living space conducive to relaxation. This could involve setting up a special nook for reading, ensuring your bedroom is reserved for sleep and relaxation only, or even creating a mini sanctuary with plants, comfortable pillows, and calming colors.
3. **Develop a Relaxing Routine**: Establish rituals that signal to your body it's time to wind down. This might include practices like yoga, meditation, or deep breathing exercises before bed. Even a simple routine of making a cup of herbal tea can help transition your mind into a state of relaxation.
4. **Digital Detox**: In our always-connected world, it's crucial to take breaks from digital devices. Set specific times when you disconnect from phones, computers, and tablets. This can reduce mental clutter and help your

mind recover from the constant bombardment of information and social media.

5. **Mindful Resting**: Active rest involves engaging in activities that are restorative rather than draining. This could be anything from a slow walk in nature to practicing mindfulness or doing gentle stretches. The key is choosing activities that refresh you rather than those that deplete your energy further.

6. **Prioritize Sleep**: While resting is not the same as sleeping, they are interconnected. Ensuring you get enough quality sleep is a foundation for good health. Invest in a good mattress, maintain a consistent sleep schedule, and create a pre-sleep routine that prepares you for a good night's rest.

7. **Listen to Your Body**: Become attuned to your body's signals. If you're feeling tired, maybe you need to slow down and rest, even if your to-do list is long. Learning to heed these signals before you're running on empty is crucial for long-term well-being.

8. **Reframe Rest**: Change how you perceive rest. It's not a sign of weakness but a sign of wisdom. Recognize that by resting, you're not only looking after yourself but also ensuring you can be your best for the people who depend on you.

9. **Teach and Model Rest for Others**: Especially if you have children, teaching them the value of rest is crucial.

They will learn how to manage their own energy and health by watching you. Model the behavior you want them to emulate, showing them that rest is a part of a healthy, balanced life.

10. **Seek Professional Help if Necessary**: If you find it difficult to allow yourself to rest due to anxiety or guilt, it might be helpful to talk to a therapist. Mental health professionals can provide strategies to manage these feelings and help you prioritize your well-being.

By incorporating these strategies, we begin to normalize and prioritize rest in our lives. It's not merely about avoiding exhaustion but about enriching our quality of life. When we are well-rested, we're not only healthier but more productive, more present, and more engaged with the world around us. Let's shed the guilt associated with taking a break and embrace the profound benefits that rest brings to our lives. Remember, taking care of yourself is not just about surviving; it's about thriving. So, dear sisters, let's commit to resting as fiercely as we do everything else in our lives. Your body, your mind, and your spirit deserve it.

"Owning our story and loving ourselves through that process is the bravest thing that we will ever do."

— BRENE BROWN

## CHAPTER 5
# God Hears You

It is hard to think that God hears you when you are having a hard time or in a storm. While praying you may ask God," Do you hear me, do you see me, do you care about what I am dealing with?" The answer to all of those questions is yes. I know how hard it is when you're praying and you feel like God isn't answering you or you don't feel heard. I have said to people in the past, "I just wish God would just tell me what to do, just talk to me like he did in biblical days". Let's be honest though, if God did tell you what he wanted you to do, would you? Or would you question it, talk to your friends and family about it, or doubt it? When we pray, God hears us. He hears us with our tears, fears, hopes, and desires. When our words fail us, God hears our hearts. God also answers us. Maybe not in the moment but He does answer. I believe that God speaks to His children differently. For me it's music. He places a song in my head and once I pay attention to the song and the "lesson" in the song He has for me, the song stops playing in my head. For someone else, it's He will speak to them through scripture. Then others simply hear His voice. I do believe that God does not speak to us in chaos. God does not yell, He whispers. Therefore He speaks to us when our minds are quiet. If you wonder if God is listening to you, pay attention when your mind is quiet, You may get the answer to your prayer. Know that your experiences, joys, and sorrows are not overlooked but cherished by God. In the vastness of the universe, you are not alone and your thoughts, dreams, and worries matter to Him. I hope this knowledge brings you peace, fortitude, and a sense of connection, knowing that you are heard, valued, and loved by our Father God. Your presence during this time is destined and part of God's plan not just for you, but for those who know you, love you, or have been influenced by you. Remember, my dear sister, that your voice is heard by a loving, compassionate Creator who only wants what is best for you.

A Creator who embraces you in his loving arms of understanding and empathy. This comforting assurance should serve as a beacon during your times of doubt and reflection. It is easy to feel isolated or forgotten when faced with life's challenges, but it is in these moments that God's presence can be most profoundly felt—if only we learn how to recognize it.

Many times, we expect direct and immediate answers. We seek signs that are as clear as day. However, God often speaks to us in subtleties that require our quiet attention and contemplation. He speaks in the stillness of our hearts, in the quiet moments when we are open to receiving His wisdom. This may come during a peaceful walk, in the silence of early morning before the world awakes, or through the words of a friend that resonate with something deeper within us.

It's also essential to recognize that God's timing differs from our own. What may seem like silence or delay is often an invitation to trust and to deepen our faith. In these periods of waiting, there is a divine purpose. They are not void of activity but are times when we are being prepared, strengthened, and aligned with God's plans for our lives which are greater and more intricate than we can understand.

Furthermore, the way we communicate with God can enhance our understanding and clarity. Prayer is not just about asking for things but also about listening. It's a two-way conversation that requires us to listen just as much as we speak. Meditation and scripture reading are practices that can help quiet the mind and open the heart, making us more receptive to God's voice.

Engaging in regular spiritual practices can strengthen our spiritual sensitivity. By setting aside dedicated time for spiritual reflection and prayer, we make room in our lives for God's voice to be heard more clearly. Whether it's through journaling, community worship, or private prayer, these practices help to anchor us in our faith and remind us of God's ever-present love. In addition to these practices, it's vital to surround ourselves with a community that uplifts and supports our spiritual journey. Being part of a faith community provides not only support but also perspectives that can help us see our situations through different lenses.

Sometimes, God uses people to deliver messages we need to hear. The encouragement, counsel, and companionship of fellow believers can be instrumental in helping us discern God's voice and direction. We should also remember that God's communication with us can be a reflection of His desire to develop certain fruits within us—patience, love, kindness, goodness, faithfulness, and self-control. Each challenge and silent period can be seen as an opportunity to cultivate these qualities, which are pleasing to God and beneficial for our growth.

It's equally important to acknowledge our role in the broader tapestry of life. Your struggles and triumphs are not just about you but also about how they equip you to assist others. You are a vessel of God's work, and your experiences enable you to empathize, support, and guide others in their spiritual walks. By recognizing this, your perspective shifts from one of individual hardship to one of collective interconnectivity, where each experience has divine significance. Lastly, take heart in knowing that God is always with you. His love is constant and unwavering. In moments of doubt, remember the biblical promise found in Deuteronomy 31:8, "The Lord himself goes before you and will be with you; he will never leave you nor forsake you. Do not be afraid; do not be discouraged." Let this verse be a source of comfort and strength.

In conclusion, remember that God hears you, sees you, and deeply cares for you. His responses to your prayers may not always come in the form you expect, but they come precisely when they need to. Continue to seek Him in the quiet, listen intently, and maintain your spiritual discipline. Above all, hold onto the faith that you are cherished, valued, and loved beyond measure by a God who is always good and who is perpetually working in your favor. May this knowledge bring you peace, hope, and an enduring sense of His presence in your life.

Here are some practical and spiritual tips for you based on the themes discussed in this chapter. These tips aim to help women foster a deeper connection with God, find peace in His presence, and navigate life's challenges with faith:

1. **Cultivate Quiet Time**: Set aside dedicated time each day for silence and solitude to listen to God's voice. Use this time for prayer, meditation, or reading scripture. Quiet moments can open your heart to deeper insights and divine whispers.
2. **Practice Active Listening in Prayer**: Instead of focusing solely on speaking during prayer, practice listening. After you share your thoughts with God, sit in silence and wait for His guidance or reassurance.
3. **Keep a Prayer Journal**: Write down your prayers, thoughts, and feelings. Over time, you can look back to see how God has moved in your life, answered your prayers, and spoken to you. This practice can strengthen your faith and provide comfort during challenging times.
4. **Join a Faith Community**: Engage with a community that supports your spiritual growth. Being part of a

church or a small group can provide spiritual encouragement, accountability, and a sense of belonging.

5. **Embrace Spiritual Disciplines**: Explore and practice spiritual disciplines like fasting, biblical study, and service. These practices can deepen your relationship with God and help you grow in your faith.

6. **Learn to Recognize God's Voice**: Familiarize yourself with the nature of God through scripture. Understanding His character and promises helps you discern His voice from your own thoughts or external influences.

7. **Trust in God's Timing**: Develop patience and trust that God's timing is perfect, even when it differs from your own expectations. Remind yourself that God sees the bigger picture and knows what is best for you.

8. **Meditate on Scripture**: Choose a verse or passage to meditate on each day. Reflecting on scripture can provide comfort, guidance, and new insights into God's will for your life.

9. **Serve Others**: Find joy and purpose in serving others. Acts of service can be a practical way to demonstrate your faith and can also be a source of spiritual fulfillment and growth.

10. **Seek Spiritual Guidance**: When you feel confused or uncertain, don't hesitate to seek guidance from a pastor, spiritual mentor, or trusted friend in your faith community.

11. **Celebrate and Reflect on Answered Prayers**: Make it a habit to celebrate when prayers are answered. Reflecting on these moments can boost your faith and gratitude during times when God seems silent.
12. **Cultivate Resilience through Faith**: Use your faith as a foundation to build resilience against life's challenges. Remember that God is with you through every trial, providing strength and comfort.
13. **Foster a Heart of Gratitude**: Even in tough times, try to find reasons to be grateful. Gratitude can shift your focus from life's hardships to its blessings, which can improve your overall sense of well-being.
14. **Share Your Testimonies**: Share stories of God's faithfulness in your life with others. Your testimonies can encourage and uplift those who hear them, and strengthen your own faith.

These tips are designed to guide women towards a fulfilling spiritual life and to help them navigate the complexities of daily living with faith and grace.

"Every great dream begins with a dreamer. Always remember, you have within you the strength, the patience, and the passion to reach for the stars to change the world."

— HARRIET TUBMAN

# CHAPTER 6
# Doubt Your Doubts and Let Go Of Your Shoulds

---

A former pastor once said in one of his sermons we had to learn to "Doubt Our Doubts". The thought of that is quite freeing. The truth is we all have doubts about our lives. We doubt our career decisions, parenting, romantic relationships, etc. They cast shadows on our capabilities. However, we need to recognize that doubts are not true indicators of our potential. I wonder what would happen if we began to doubt our doubts. Ignoring the little negative voice in your head causes you to doubt what you want and need. "I want to go back to school, but I don't think I can." "I want to look for a new job, but I'm not sure if I should." Notice the common word in both of these sentences is "but". The "but" is what causes you to doubt yourself. When the "but" enters your mind replace it with a "why". "Why shouldn't I go back to school"? "Why shouldn't I look for a new job?" Then there are the people who put doubts in your mind, The ones who tell you things like, "We don't know anyone who has done that before".

"No one in our family has ever done that, why do you think you can?" Don't allow anyone's doubt to become your doubt. Their doubt and fear about what you're doing should not become yours. Society tries to project expectations onto you. However, your journey is yours and yours alone. Society may try to use racism or misogyny to cast doubt but again doubt it. Society's limitation belongs to society, it doesn't have to belong to you unless you allow it to. You are a unique individual with a unique gift and talent, embrace it. Letting go of your shoulds can be just as difficult as doubting your doubts. Let me explain the shoulds. Have you ever looked at your life and compared it to someone else's and said, "I should be doing that?" Or looked at your life and said, "I should be in a different place at this point in my life?" I have. I did that just the other day. I think we all feel that way at times. The truth is though you SHOULD be exactly where you are at this moment. Letting go of the shoulds doesn't mean you don't stop trying to be better or become complacent. It means you stop comparing yourself to others. When you're always saying what you SHOULD have or where you SHOULD be, you don't appreciate where you are. If you don't appreciate where you are, how will you know or appreciate when you reach a SHOULD? The truth is when we say where we should be or what we should be doing, we are doing the new version of "keeping up with the Joneses." Your journey is purely your own. Focus on that and you may get your SHOULDS, or get better than your SHOULDS.

The truth is when we say where we should be or what we should be doing, we are doing the new version of "keeping up with the Joneses." Your journey is purely your own. Focus on that and you may get your SHOULDS, or get better than your SHOULDS.

When we internalize this mindset, we free ourselves from the crippling weight of unrealistic expectations and societal pressures. We enable ourselves to live more authentically and pursue our true passions and purposes without the constant comparison that can cloud our judgment and dampen our spirits.

## Breaking Free from Social Comparisons

It's imperative to acknowledge the role of social media and societal pressures in shaping our perceptions of success and achievement. The curated lives we see online can often make us feel as if we are not achieving enough, fast enough. This digital illusion can skew our understanding of real progress and personal growth. It's crucial to recognize that each post, image, or story is merely a snapshot, not the full picture of someone's life. Thus, detaching from these comparisons is vital.

## Embracing Your Unique Path

Embracing your unique path means understanding and accepting that your life is not meant to mimic anyone else's. This acceptance is liberating and allows you to explore what truly makes you happy, fulfilled, and motivated. Ask yourself what you value most, what brings you joy, and what you are passionate about. Let these answers guide your decisions rather than the overshadowing shoulds imposed by external comparisons.

## Cultivating Self-Confidence

Cultivating a strong sense of self-confidence is fundamental in doubting your doubts. Self-confidence stems not from the absence of doubt but from the ability to move forward despite it. Building this confidence involves setting and achieving small, manageable goals. Each accomplishment, no matter how minor it may seem, is a building block in the robust structure of your self-assurance.

## Focusing on Personal Growth

Instead of fixating on where you think you should be, focus on how far you've come and where you can go. Personal growth is an ongoing process, not a destination. It's about becoming a better version of yourself, step by step. Set personal goals that challenge you but are also achievable. Celebrate your progress regularly, and use setbacks as learning experiences.

## Practicing Mindfulness and Gratitude

Mindfulness and gratitude can shift your perspective from what you lack to what you possess. Practicing mindfulness involves being present in the moment and appreciating it without judgment. Gratitude, on the other hand, involves recognizing and appreciating the value of what you have. These practices can significantly diminish the power of doubts and shoulds, enhancing your emotional and mental well-being.

## Seeking Support

No journey should be walked alone. Seeking support from trusted friends, mentors, or professionals can provide encouragement, advice, and new perspectives. These relationships can fortify your resolve to pursue your path and help you navigate the complexities of life's decisions.

## Educating Yourself

Education is a powerful tool in overcoming doubts. Whether formal or informal, gaining knowledge and skills in areas of interest builds competence and confidence. Education expands your horizons, opens new doors, and can significantly diminish feelings of inadequacy and doubt.

## Letting Go of Perfectionism

Perfectionism is often the root of many doubts. It sets an impossibly high standard that is both unrealistic and unattainable. Learning to let go of the need for perfection and embracing excellence as a more flexible goal can reduce stress and make your objectives more achievable.

## Living Intentionally

Living intentionally means making choices that align with your core values, aspirations, and authentic self. It means living by design, not by default. Making intentional choices helps you lead a more purposeful and satisfying life, reducing the influence of doubts that stem from external sources.

**Reflecting Regularly**

Regular reflection allows you to evaluate your experiences, learn from them, and make informed decisions moving forward. It's a practice that helps you understand your motivations, reassess your goals, and realign your actions with your true self.

By implementing these practices, you can begin to doubt your doubts more effectively. You learn to trust yourself and your instincts, making decisions that are right for you, not just those that appear right to others. This journey of self-discovery and empowerment is not about reaching a destination but about embracing each step of the path with confidence and grace.

In conclusion, remember that doubting your doubts isn't about ignoring them; it's about challenging them to ensure they don't hold you back. It's about understanding your worth, recognizing your potential, and taking control of your narrative. As you continue to grow and evolve, let the freedom from these doubts guide you to a fuller, more authentic life. Remember, in the end, your journey is about creating a story that you are proud to tell—one that is uniquely and unmistakably yours.

Here are some more practical and empowering tips for you based on the themes discussed in this chapter. These tips are designed to help women build confidence, embrace their unique paths, and doubt their doubts effectively:

1. **Define Your Values**: Understand what truly matters to you. Define your core values and let them guide your decisions and actions. This clarity will help you navigate life with purpose and ward off doubts that arise from external pressures.
2. **Set Achievable Goals**: Break your larger goals into smaller, manageable steps. Achieving these can boost your confidence and provide tangible evidence of your capabilities, which helps in doubting your doubts.
3. **Practice Mindfulness**: Engage in mindfulness practices daily. Whether it's meditation, deep breathing, or simply being present in the moment, mindfulness helps reduce stress and quieten the negative voices in your head.
4. **Cultivate Gratitude**: Keep a gratitude journal or make it a habit to acknowledge what you are thankful for each day. This practice shifts your focus from what's lacking to what's abundant in your life.
5. **Seek Supportive Relationships**: Surround yourself with people who uplift you. Having a supportive network can strengthen your resolve to pursue your goals and provide reassurance when doubts creep in.
6. **Embrace Lifelong Learning**: Commit to continuous learning and self-improvement. Whether it's taking a new

class, reading, or exploring a new hobby, education enhances your self-esteem and equips you with new skills.

7. **Let Go of Perfectionism**: Aim for excellence, not perfection. Recognize that making mistakes is a part of learning and growth. Perfectionism can paralyze progress; embracing imperfection allows you to move forward more freely.

8. **Live Intentionally**: Make conscious choices that align with your personal values and goals. Living intentionally prevents you from being swayed by others' expectations or societal pressures.

9. **Regular Self-Reflection**: Allocate time regularly to reflect on your experiences. Self-reflection helps you understand your motivations, celebrate your successes, and learn from your setbacks.

10. **Normalize Self-Care**: Prioritize self-care as essential, not optional. Proper self-care enhances your overall well-being, making you more resilient against doubts and stress.

11. **Challenge Negative Thoughts**: When doubts arise, challenge them with evidence of your past successes and strengths. This can help reshape your thought patterns from self-doubt to self-assurance.

12. **Celebrate Your Unique Journey**: Acknowledge and celebrate your unique path. Understand that everyone's journey is different, and comparing yourself to others is not only unproductive but also misleading.

13. **Develop Emotional Resilience**: Work on building your emotional resilience by facing challenges head-on and learning to recover from setbacks. Resilience is key to maintaining your course despite the doubts that may arise.
14. **Be Your Own Advocate**: Stand up for yourself and your needs in both personal and professional settings. Being your own advocate reinforces your sense of self-worth and helps silence internal and external doubts.

By incorporating these tips into your daily life, you can empower yourself to doubt your doubts and embrace a more confident, fulfilled, and authentic existence. Remember, every step you take in doubting your doubts is a step towards realizing your true potential.

"I learned that courage was not the absence of fear, but the triumph over it. The brave man is not he who does not feel afraid, but he who conquers that fear."

— NELSON MANDELA

## CHAPTER 7
# Go After Your Dreams

What did you want to be when you grew up? I wanted to be a singer. Music was my life for the longest time. Although I still love to sing and I believe music is life it is no longer my life. It's no longer my life because I found my gift, therapy. I used to watch the show "Growing Pains" as a teen and say to myself, "That's what I want to do." I knew at 14 I wanted to be a therapist, a singing therapist at that. Becoming a therapist became my dream. Achieving that dream wasn't easy but it wasn't supposed to be. Dreams with work become a goal. Dreams without work become a wish. They both start with a dream. At the end of the day, I would do it all over again. The first thing you should do is know who you are and what you want from your dream. Celebrate your uniqueness and allow it to navigate the path to your dreams. Take the time to define your dream, not your family, friends, or society's expectations. There are many miserable people in the world because they are living someone else's dreams instead of their own. What an awful existence. Your dreams should resonate with your authentic self and it should fuel you.

When going after your dream, you will be faced with obstacles. Look at the obstacles as a learning experience and a chance to grow. When you find yourself dealing with an obstacle or obstacles, rise above it with resilience. Another way to go after your dreams is by having a support system that holds you accountable and celebrates you. Build relationships with like-minded people who will encourage you and you encourage them with their dreams. Having people in your life who are jealous or unsupporting will only frustrate you and make you feel alone. When going after your dreams, it is important to celebrate your wins. It doesn't matter how big or small your win is. Use your achievements as a reminder of where you've been and where you're going. You are the author of your success story. Sis, the world is waiting for you and your greatness. Your dreams are valid, your journey is significant and you have limitless potential. Keep going for your dreams. Be bold, be brave, have audacity, and believe in yourself and your ability to achieve your dream. Don't let your biggest regret that you allowed your dream to become a wish.

## Unleashing Your Potential

At the core of chasing dreams is the belief in oneself. This belief acts as the fuel that propels you forward, even when the path is obscured by doubts or obstacles. It's about embracing the notion that your potential is not fixed but boundless, capable of expansion and growth through persistence and experience.

## Establishing Clear Goals

Define your dreams clearly and set specific, measurable, attainable, relevant, and time-bound (SMART) goals. This clarity transforms a vague dream into a series of actionable steps. When you know exactly what you are working towards, each step becomes intentional and each milestone, a celebration.

## Continuous Learning and Adaptation

The journey towards realizing your dreams is often nonlinear. It involves learning from every experience and adapting your strategies as needed. Continuous learning can come from formal education, self-study, mentorship, and even from failures. Each lesson refines your approach and sharpens your understanding of your own capabilities and the landscape around you.

## Overcoming Fear and Embracing Risk

Fear is often the greatest barrier to achieving dreams. It can paralyze you into inaction or make you overly cautious. It's essential to recognize that fear of failure is a common experience—an experience not to be shunned but embraced. Learn to view risk as a necessary element of success. Taking calculated risks can lead to substantial rewards and push you closer to your dreams.

## Building and Leveraging Your Network

Your network can provide support, advice, opportunities, and motivation necessary for the pursuit of your dreams. Build relationships with individuals who inspire you, who challenge you, and who bring out the best in you. Surround yourself with positivity and expertise, and don't hesitate to reach out for help when you need it.

## Maintaining Resilience

The path to achieving your dreams is often strewn with challenges that test your resilience. Developing a resilient mindset involves understanding that setbacks are not endpoints but part of the learning curve. Embrace resilience by setting aside time for reflection, allowing yourself to process and learn from each situation.

## Prioritizing Self-Care

While pursuing your dreams, it's crucial to maintain your physical, mental, and emotional health. Neglecting self-care can lead to burnout, which can derail your efforts. Establish routines that prioritize your well-being, including adequate sleep, nutrition, exercise, and relaxation. Remember, a well-rested mind is more creative and more efficient.

## Celebrating Every Victory

No matter how small, every victory on the path to your dream is worth celebrating. These celebrations reinforce positive emotions and can boost your motivation. They remind you of the progress you've made and why you started this journey in the first place.

## Staying True to Your Authentic Self

In the pursuit of dreams, it's easy to lose sight of who you are and what you truly want. Always ensure that your path aligns with your values and the essence of who you are. Compromising your authenticity for success or approval from others can lead to dissatisfaction and regret.

## Using Visualizations and Affirmations

Visualize your success and use affirmations to reinforce your capability to achieve your dreams. This practice can boost your confidence and help maintain a positive and focused mindset.

## Being Patient and Persistent

Understand that dreams do not materialize overnight. Patience is essential, as is persistence. There will be days when progress seems slow or nonexistent, but these are the days when your commitment to your dreams is truly tested.

## Adjusting Expectations

Be flexible with your expectations. As you grow and evolve, so too may your dreams. Be open to exploring new paths or adjusting your goals as you gain more insight and experience.

## Leaving a Legacy

Think about the legacy you want to leave. How do you want to be remembered? By aligning your actions with the legacy you wish to leave, you give your dreams a deeper purpose. This legacy-oriented thinking can provide a powerful motivation that transcends personal success.

In conclusion, chasing your dreams is about much more than merely achieving goals. It's about the growth you experience along the way, the people you inspire, and the fulfillment that comes from pursuing what truly matters to you. Always remember that your dreams are a reflection of your deepest desires and potential. Be fearless in your pursuit, unwavering in your commitment, and dedicated to the journey of becoming who you are meant to be. Remember, every step forward is a step towards realizing the incredible possibilities that your unique gifts and talents can bring to the world. Let your dreams be your guide, and let your spirit be free to explore the heights it was meant to reach.

Here are some additional helpful tips for women based on the information you've taken in throughout this chapter. These tips offer more insights and strategies for pursuing personal dreams and achieving greater self-fulfillment:

1. **Embrace Imperfection**: Understand that the journey towards your dreams is not about perfection. Embrace your imperfections as part of your unique story. Accepting that you are a work in progress allows you to move forward with more confidence and less fear of making mistakes.
2. **Practice Intentional Daily Actions**: Every day, take small, intentional actions that align with your long-term

goals. This consistency turns small efforts into big achievements over time and helps maintain your momentum.

3. **Seek Diverse Perspectives**: Expand your viewpoints by seeking out advice and insights from people outside your usual circle. Diverse perspectives can inspire innovative solutions to obstacles and enrich your journey.

4. **Create a Vision Board**: Visualize your goals by creating a vision board that represents your dreams through images and phrases. This visual representation can serve as a daily reminder and motivation of what you're working towards.

5. **Limit Social Media Consumption**: Be mindful of the time you spend on social media and the content you consume. It's important to stay connected, but too much exposure can lead to comparison and discouragement.

6. **Develop a Growth Mindset**: Cultivate a growth mindset by believing that your abilities and intelligence can be developed through dedication and hard work. This perspective encourages a love of learning and a resilience that is essential for great accomplishment.

7. **Set Healthy Financial Goals**: Financial independence is crucial for empowerment. Set and pursue financial goals that support your dreams, such as saving for further education, starting a business, or funding a creative project.

8. **Volunteer Your Time**: Engage in volunteer work that aligns with your passions or career goals. Volunteering can expand your network, increase your skills, and provide new experiences that enrich your personal and professional life.

9. **Negotiate for What You Deserve**: Whether it's salary, project opportunities, or professional roles, don't be afraid to negotiate for what you deserve. Understanding your value and advocating for yourself are key components of achieving your dreams.

10. **Maintain Work-Life Balance**: Strive to find a balance that allows you to be productive without compromising your well-being. A well-balanced life enhances creativity and endurance in pursuing your goals.

11. **Reflect on Your Journey Regularly**: Take time regularly to reflect on your journey. Consider what you've learned, how you've grown, and what you can improve. This reflection can provide valuable insights that guide your future actions.

12. **Learn to Say No**: Protect your time and energy by learning to say no to demands that do not serve your goals or align with your priorities. This helps you stay focused on your path and prevents burnout.

13. **Celebrate Other Women**: Support and celebrate the achievements of other women. A supportive community

fosters a network of encouragement and inspiration, which is beneficial for everyone involved.

By integrating these tips into your life, you can enhance your ability to pursue your dreams with vigor and clarity. Each tip is designed to empower you, helping to build the resilience, skills, and mindset needed to navigate the challenges and seize the opportunities that come your way.

"You gain strength, courage, and confidence by every experience in which you really stop to look fear in the face. You are able to say to yourself, 'I have lived through this horror. I can take the next thing that comes along."

— ELEANOR ROOSEVELT

## CHAPTER 8
# Healed And Healing

Letting go of a past pain that still hurts you emotionally is not something that just happens. It's not an easy thing to do. Even the healing process is painful. However, the pain of the heal is better than the pain of the injury. Some people would rather sit with the pain of the injury simply because they become used to that pain and they're afraid of the pain of the heal. Think about surgery. A person has surgery because something is wrong. Once the surgery is done the doctor will put stitches in the incision but what they fixed on the inside also has to heal. While the incision may be healed, what was fixed internally is still healing. During the healing process, the stitches may begin to itch, and there may be bruising but there is still healing happening. Being healed is not something you do for someone else. It's a gift that you give to yourself. Because once you have healed from one thing, you can begin to work on healing from something else. Being healed and healing allows you to grow and move forward. It's freeing. It frees you from the pain but it also frees you from the people in your life who don't want you to heal. I am sure you can think of a person or two who only want you to be unhealed because they are unhealed. As the old saying goes, "Misery loves company." Being healed and healing is scary. In many ways, you're stepping out of your comfort zone. We get used to the injury and the dysfunction that we don't realize there is a better to feel, think, and be better. The most important thing about being healed and healing is forgiveness. Forgiving yourself for not treating yourself with love, grace, and kindness. Then forgive the person or people who injured you physically, emotionally, financially, etc. The hardest one of these is forgiving yourself. Sometimes the first step in healing is permitting yourself TO HEAL. I know some of you are saying, "Permit myself to heal?" Yes. Sometimes we are the reason we aren't healing. We feel guilty about healing, leaving others in their pain while we heal from ours. The truth is healing is a very personal journey. It's a journey everyone is not ready to do. Therefore, you have to make the decision to work on your healing even if that means leaving people that you love behind.

Yes, sometimes we are the reason we aren't healing. We feel guilty about healing, leaving others in their pain while we heal from ours. The truth is, that healing is a very personal journey. It's a journey everyone is not ready to do.

## The Power of Setting Boundaries

One of the fundamental aspects of healing is learning to set boundaries. This can be extremely challenging, especially if you are accustomed to prioritizing others' needs over your own.

Setting boundaries is crucial for your mental health; it helps you respect yourself and requires others to respect your space and your healing process. When you establish clear boundaries, you create a safe environment for yourself to grow and heal.

## The Role of Self-Compassion

Healing also requires a great deal of self-compassion. It's about being kind to yourself during moments of pain or setbacks. Self-compassion involves acknowledging your suffering, recognizing that suffering is a part of life, and being kind to yourself as you navigate your healing journey. This can involve practical steps like speaking to yourself kindly, allowing yourself time to rest and recover, and engaging in activities that nourish your soul and body.

## Finding the Right Support System

While healing is a personal journey, having a support system can provide additional strength and perspective. This doesn't necessarily mean always seeking support from friends or family who may be dealing with their own issues. Sometimes, it involves professional help such as therapists or counselors who are trained to guide you through the healing process. Other times, it might involve community groups or online forums where people share similar experiences.

### Engaging in Therapeutic Practices

Engaging in therapeutic practices can significantly aid your healing process. This might include therapy, but it can also involve practices like meditation, yoga, art therapy, or writing. These activities help by providing outlets for expression and processing emotions, and they can also help to center and calm your mind, making it easier to cope with the challenges of healing.

### Embracing Change and Growth

Healing is not just about returning to how things were before the pain. It's about growth and often transformation. Embrace the changes that come with healing; recognize that you may emerge with a new perspective on life, new strengths, and perhaps a new direction. Healing can redefine who you are, and while this can be frightening, it can also be profoundly liberating.

### Forgiving as a Path to Healing

As previously mentioned, forgiveness is vital in the healing process. This includes forgiving others and forgiving yourself. Forgiveness does not mean forgetting or excusing the harm done to you, but rather letting go of the grip that pain has on your heart. Holding onto resentment or anger ties you to the past and hinders your healing. Forgiveness is a challenging journey, but it is also a powerful step toward reclaiming your freedom and peace.

## Celebrating Small Wins

It's important to recognize and celebrate small wins on your journey to healing. Acknowledging progress, no matter how minor, can provide motivation to continue and can serve as a reminder of the growth that is occurring even when it feels slow or painful. Celebrating these victories can reinforce a positive mindset and help sustain your healing momentum.

## Reflecting on Your Journey

Take time to reflect on your healing journey. This can involve journaling your thoughts and feelings, reflecting on what you've learned, and contemplating how you've changed. Reflection can help solidify the lessons of the journey and can provide a clearer understanding of the path forward.

## Knowing When to Let Go

Part of healing is knowing when to let go—whether it's letting go of toxic relationships, unhealthy habits, or old grudges that hold you back. Letting go is not a sign of weakness; it's a sign of strength and an essential part of healing.

## Rebuilding Confidence

As you heal, work on rebuilding your confidence which might have been shaken by your experiences. Engage in activities that strengthen your sense of self-worth. Celebrate your unique qualities and talents, and set goals that challenge you to harness your potential.

## Navigating Relapses

Understand that healing is not linear. There may be times when old wounds resurface. This is a normal part of the healing process. When this happens, treat yourself with kindness, reach out for support if needed, and use the coping strategies you've developed.

*Heal My Sister, Heal.*

In this journey, it is vital to recognize that healing often requires layers of unlearning and relearning. The process involves stripping away the burdens that have been borne out of past traumas, societal expectations, or personal disappointments. It's about peeling back these layers to reveal a more authentic self, one that is capable of experiencing joy, peace, and fulfillment.

## Embracing the New

Embracing the new is about more than just adopting new behaviors; it's about opening your life to new possibilities, experiences, and ways of being. It means allowing yourself to be vulnerable and to step into spaces and relationships that nurture your growth. It's about finding joy in the unexpected and learning to trust the journey, even when the destination isn't clear.

## Letting Go of the Old

Letting go is often one of the hardest parts of healing because it requires you to release things that may once have given you comfort or identity. This could be toxic relationships, self-destructive habits, or outdated self-perceptions. Letting go involves a deep level of forgiveness and acceptance. It's about understanding that holding onto past pain doesn't serve your present or your future. It means forgiving not only those who have hurt you but also forgiving yourself for the times you didn't live up to your own expectations.

## The Power of Saying No—and Yes

A crucial part of healing is learning when to say no, and when to say yes. Saying no to others can be difficult, especially for those who have spent a lifetime prioritizing the needs and wants of others over their own. But every no to something that doesn't serve you is a yes to something that does. It is a yes to self-care, to personal boundaries, and to your own health and well-being.

On the flip side, saying yes to yourself is an act of profound self-love. It means saying yes to opportunities that excite you, relationships that support you, and dreams that inspire you. It's about making choices that align with your deepest values and desires, and courageously pursuing what truly makes you feel alive and connected to your purpose.

## Starting Over

There's a profound strength in the ability to start over. It's a declaration that your past does not define your future. Starting over might mean revisiting old goals with new strategies or completely changing your direction in life. It's about giving yourself permission to pursue happiness and fulfillment, regardless of age, circumstance, or the amount of time you've spent on a different path.

## The Marathon of Healing

Remember, healing is a marathon, not a sprint. It doesn't adhere to a timeline, and there will be days when progress feels slow or nonexistent. On these days, it's important to remind yourself of how far you've come and to celebrate even the smallest victories. Healing requires patience, persistence, and a gentle but unwavering commitment to self-care and self-compassion.

In conclusion, as you continue on your healing journey, hold onto the belief that each step forward, no matter how small, is a step toward a healthier, more fulfilled you. Heal, my sister, heal—not just for you but for the vibrant life that awaits you beyond your healing.

In conclusion, healing from past pain is a deeply personal, often complex journey that requires courage, commitment, and patience. It involves embracing vulnerability, setting boundaries, and often changing the dynamics of existing relationships. The path to healing isn't easy, but it is rich with opportunities for personal growth and transformation. Remember, each step taken is a step toward a more liberated, authentic life where you are not defined by your past, but informed by it. Continue to persevere with compassion and courage

# EXERCISES

*Here are 25 self-help exercises designed specifically for women, each with detailed instructions and practical takeaways to help encourage personal growth, self-awareness, and emotional well-being*

EXERCISES

# 01
# Gratitude Journaling

**Instructions:**

Every morning or evening, write down three things you are grateful for in a dedicated journal. These can be big or small—from a good cup of coffee to a meaningful conversation with a friend.

**Takeaway:**

Regular gratitude journaling can shift your focus from what you lack to what you possess, fostering a positive mindset and increasing overall happiness.

# 02
## Mindful Meditation

**Instructions:**

Set aside 10-15 minutes daily to meditate. Find a quiet space, sit comfortably, and focus on your breath. When your mind wanders, gently bring your attention back to your breathing.

**Takeaway:**

Mindful meditation can reduce stress, improve concentration, and enhance your overall emotional resilience, helping you remain centered in daily life.

EXERCISES

# 03
# The "No" Exercise

### Instructions:

For one week, practice saying no to things that don't align with your personal goals or drain your energy. Note how you feel each time you assertively say no.

### Takeaway:

This exercise helps reinforce your boundaries, teaching you the importance of prioritizing your needs and mental health.

## 04
# Future Self Visualization

**Instructions:**

Spend 10 minutes visualizing where you want to be in five years. Be detailed about your career, lifestyle, and relationships. Write down your vision and the steps you think will get you there.

**Takeaway:**

Visualization can motivate you and clarify the direction you need to take to achieve your dreams, enhancing your goal-setting and planning skills.

EXERCISES

## 05
## Self-Compassion Pause

**Instructions:**

Whenever you catch yourself being critical, pause. Place a hand on your heart and say a compassionate phrase to yourself, like "I am doing my best," or "I forgive myself."

**Takeaway:**

This exercise helps develop self-compassion, reducing negative self-talk and increasing emotional resilience.

# 06
# Strengths Assessment

### Instructions:

Write a list of your personal strengths and three ways you can use each strength in your current life situation. Ask friends or family to add to the list if you're stuck.

### Takeaway:

Recognizing and utilizing your strengths can boost self-confidence and ensure you are leveraging your best attributes in all areas of life.

## 07
# Emotional Check-In

**Instructions:**

Set a daily reminder to check in with your emotions. Identify how you're feeling at that moment and why. Acknowledge each emotion without judgment and write them down if helpful.

**Takeaway:**

Regular emotional check-ins can enhance emotional intelligence, helping you better manage your reactions and deepen your understanding of yourself.

## 08
# The Letter of Forgiveness

**Instructions:**

Write a letter of forgiveness to someone who has wronged you in the past, including forgiving yourself if applicable. You do not need to send it; the act is for your emotional release.

**Takeaway:**

Forgiveness can significantly lighten your emotional load, leading to healing and closure from past hurts.

EXERCISES

## 09
## Daily Affirmations

**Instructions:**

Begin each morning by saying out loud three affirmations that reinforce positive self-identity, such as "I am capable," "I am worthy of respect," or "I embrace my power."

**Takeaway:**

Positive affirmations can boost your self-esteem and change negative thought patterns into empowering beliefs.

# 10
# Physical Activity Goal

**Instructions:**

Set a realistic weekly physical activity goal. This could be walking a certain number of steps, attending yoga classes, or engaging in any physical activity that you enjoy.

**Takeaway:**

Regular physical activity can improve both physical and mental health, boosting your mood and reducing symptoms of anxiety and depression.

# 11
# Art Expression

**Instructions:**

Allocate time each week to express yourself creatively through art. This can be painting, drawing, crafting, or any other form of art that feels therapeutic.

**Takeaway:**

Artistic expression can be a profound way to process and express emotions that might be difficult to articulate verbally.

# 12
## Sleep Hygiene Practice

**Instructions:**

Develop a nightly routine that promotes good sleep hygiene—this might include dimming the lights, turning off screens an hour before bed, and using relaxation techniques.

**Takeaway:**

Improving sleep hygiene can significantly impact your overall health, mood, and cognitive function.

## 13

# Social Media Detox

**Instructions:**

Plan a weekend or a full week where you significantly reduce or completely abstain from using social media.

**Takeaway:**

A break from social media can decrease stress and promote a greater sense of present-moment awareness in your daily life.

# 14
# Nutrition Journal

## Instructions:

Keep a food diary for one week, noting everything you eat and how it makes you feel physically and emotionally.

## Takeaway:

Monitoring your eating habits can help you identify foods that affect your mood and energy levels, leading to better nutritional choices.

EXERCISES

# 15
## Letting Go Ritual

**Instructions:**

Write down a list of past grievances or regrets, read them aloud in a private, comfortable space, and then safely burn the paper as a symbolic release.

**Takeaway:**

Engaging in a letting go ritual can help close old wounds and reaffirm your commitment to moving forward.

# 16
## Positive Networking

**Instructions:**

Join a group or club that aligns with your interests or goals. Make an effort to connect with new people and build supportive relationships.

**Takeaway:**

Expanding your social network can introduce you to new ideas and supportive relationships that empower your personal growth.

EXERCISES

# 17
# Personal Development Book Club

**Instructions:**

Start or join a book club focused on personal development and healing. Discuss the books and share insights with club members.

**Takeaway:**

Reading and discussing personal development books can provide new tools for healing and personal growth, and discussing them can deepen your understanding and motivation.

# 18
# Weekly Self-Care Appointment

**Instructions:**

Schedule a weekly "appointment" dedicated to self-care. This could be a spa day, a long walk in nature, or an hour spent in a favorite cafe.

**Takeaway:**

Regularly scheduled self-care reinforces the importance of taking time to recharge and can significantly improve your overall well-being.

EXERCISES

# 19
## Journal of Achievements

**Instructions:**

Maintain a journal where you record all your achievements, big or small, as they occur throughout the year.

**Takeaway:**

Keeping a record of your achievements can boost your confidence and motivate you to pursue bigger goals.

# 20
# Assertiveness Training

**Instructions:**

Practice assertiveness by expressing your thoughts and needs directly and respectfully in your interactions.

**Takeaway:**

Developing assertiveness can improve your relationships and help you establish respect and clear boundaries.

## 21
# Life Vision Board

**Instructions:**

Create a vision board that represents your goals and aspirations in all areas of your life using images and words from magazines or printed from online sources.

**Takeaway:**

A vision board can keep you inspired and focused on your life goals, making them more tangible and attainable.

# 22
# Grounding Techniques

**Instructions:**

Learn and practice grounding techniques, such as the "5-4-3-2-1" method, which involves identifying things you can see, touch, hear, smell, and taste to bring your attention to the present.

**Takeaway:**

Grounding techniques can be particularly helpful in managing anxiety and stress, helping you stay centered during challenging times.

EXERCISES

# 23
# Kindness Challenge

**Instructions:**

Commit to performing a small act of kindness each day for a month. This could be as simple as giving a compliment, holding a door open, or sending an encouraging text.

**Takeaway:**

Acts of kindness can increase your sense of connection to others and boost your mood.

# 24
## Career Advancement Steps

**Instructions:**

Identify and take at least one small step each month to advance your career, whether it's learning a new skill, updating your resume, or networking with peers.

**Takeaway:**

Proactively taking steps to advance your career can boost your professional confidence and open up new opportunities.

# 25
# Mindful Listening Practice

**Instructions:**

Engage in at least one conversation per day where you practice fully focusing on the other person, without planning your response while they speak.

**Takeaway:**

Mindful listening can improve your relationships and communication skills, leading to deeper connections and understanding.

# ABOUT THE AUTHOR

Adawna Bell is a beacon of hope and healing in the field of Social Services, where she has dedicated over two decades to nurturing families and guiding them toward a path of reconciliation and emotional well-being. Adawna has embraced the entrepreneurial spirit, founding her practice, After Happily Ever After, where she continues to inspire positive change in the lives of those she works with. Adawna's academic background is as impressive as her professional journey. She obtained her Bachelor of Science in Psychology from the University of Connecticut in 1999 and later, her Master of Science in Marriage and Family Therapy from Nova Southeastern University in 2009. A licensed Marriage and Family Therapist in both Florida and Alabama, and a Qualified Supervisor in Florida, Adawna's credentials are a testament to her commitment to her field. She is the mother of two amazing children and honors the life of her late husband whom she shared 24 years of marriage.

Learn more about Adawna at:
www.afterhappilyeverafter.org

For bookings, appearances and bulk book sales please contact:

Build A Brother Publishing
support@buildabrother.com

www.ingramcontent.com/pod-product-compliance
Lightning Source LLC
Chambersburg PA
CBHW072050160426
43197CB00014B/2698